A Growing Light

Advent Meditations

John L. Hoh, Jr.

ISBN: 978-1-105-25721-6

HoneyMilk Publications
An imprint of H2O Scrolls & Codices
4859 N. 78th St.
Milwaukee WI 53218

Contents

Overview: What is Advent?

At the beginning of a new church year is a season called Advent. "Advent" comes from a Latin word meaning "to arrive." It commemorates the Old Testament believers awaiting the arrival of the promised Messiah, the Christ.

New Testament believers also use this time to reflect on our own wait for an arrival—the arrival of our Lord for the final Judgment. As such the season before Christmas can take on eschatological overtones.

A tradition among Christians, especially among the Catholic, Orthodox, and Lutheran traditions, is to have meditations with an advent wreath. This wreath is a circle of evergreen boughs. Four candles, sometimes five, adorn the wreath. These candles can have differing meanings depending upon which series of meditations is followed.

The wreath with evergreen boughs represents eternal life. The wreath's circle reflects God eternal nature—no beginning and no ending.

The candles reflect the coming light of the world. As such the season leads to the Winter Solstice, a date when the days start to get longer. They will eventually "lengthen" in Lent (which is where that term comes from). As the Christian progresses through Advent more candles are lit. And thus we have *A Growing Light*. There are as many as five candles. Four rest around the wreath. One sits in the center.

The colors of the candles vary with different traditions, but there are usually three purple or blue candles, corresponding to the sanctuary colors of Advent, and one pink or rose candle. One of the purple candles is lighted the first Sunday of Advent, a Scripture is read, a short devotional or reading is given, and a prayer offered. On subsequent Sundays, previous candles are relighted with an additional one lighted. The pink/rose candle is usually lit on the third Sunday of Advent.

The following table lists the possible names for the candles.

Meaning	**Candle 1**	**Candle 2**	**Candle 3**	**Candle 4**
Advent Actions	Expectation	Annunciation	Proclamation	Fulfillment
Nativity Principles	Mary	Shepherds	Joseph	Wise Men
Promise Messengers	Prophecy	Bethlehem	Shepherds	Angels
	Prophets	John the Baptis	Mary	Magi
	Prophets	Angels	Shepherds	Wise Men
Fruits of Spirit	Hope	Peace	Love	Joy
	Faith	Joy	Love	Hope
Salvation Cycle	History	New Birth	2nd Coming	Peace

Advent: The Start of a New Church Year

Let me be the first to wish you a Happy New Year! Happy New Year?

John, aren't you jumping the gun here? New Year's is almost a month away yet!

No, I haven't taken leave of my senses. Generally right after Thanksgiving a new church year starts. This season, four weeks before Christmas, is known as "Advent." Literally, "advent" comes from the Latin "*advenio*," meaning "to come." It is the season when we await the birth of the Messiah as the Old Testament believers awaited. It is also a time when we await the return of our Lord for Judgment. In a sense, this season does continue many of the themes of the last three Sundays of Pentecost-the end times and the coming Judgment.

The Lutheran church is a liturgical church. As such, it is often seen as "like the Catholics." Luther retained much of what the Church had in his reforms-he didn't throw the baby out with the bath water. As such, as the seasons arrive this coming Church year, I will highlight each season in this forum. This forum has posted an overview of the Church year in the past-feel free to read that overview.

The liturgical colors of Advent are currently light blue. Purple-for penitence-used to be the liturgical color, but now the focus of the season is no longer strictly on penitence but now also looks forward to our heavenly home.

The season also looks at the prophecies of the coming Messiah and how the impending birth fulfilled those prophecies.

Traditionally, four candles are lit in an Advent wreath. Week one sees one candle lit, week two sees two lit candles, and so forth. In the middle is a white candle—the Christ candle-which is lit on Christmas. There are several meanings attributed to the four candles. Some traditions for the candles include:

Tradition One (Anglican)

The individual candles (from left to right) represent:

1. First Sunday: The first candle reminds us of the patriarchs, Abraham and David, the Old Testament ancestors of Jesus.
2. Second Sunday: The second candle reminds us of the prophets, who foretold the birth of Jesus.
3. Third Sunday: The third candle reminds us of John the Baptist, who proclaimed and baptized Jesus in the Jordan.
4. Fourth Sunday: The fourth candle reminds us of the Virgin who bore

Jesus in her womb.

5. 25th December: The fifth candle reminds of the birth of Jesus, God become man.

Now we'll light the candles, Candles in a ring;
So that they will light the way
For our coming King.
Ev'ry year they help us count
By their bright array
And remember why Christ came On that Christmas Day! Thinking of God's promise
As we light the first: Darkness He will overthrow
For our God is just! Jesus is our only light
And through Him we pray
And remember why Christ came
On that Christmas Day!

Prophets with a message
Of how Christ would come To redeem a fallen world; Calling us back home.
Guide us by this candle's flame;
May we never stray
But remember why Christ came
On that Christmas Day!

John's voice in the desert
Said: "Christ's way prepare;
Crooked roads must be made straight, Or God's wrath you'll share!"
Help us to repent our sins; Light for us a way

To remember why Christ came
On that Christmas Day!

Mary was so willing; Bearing God's own Son: Only by this Gift to us
Was our pardon won.
These four candles help us think
Of debts we can't repay
And remember why Christ came
On that Christmas Day! ADVENT CANDLES

Tradition Two

ADVENT RING LIGHTING CEREMONY
THE FIRST SUNDAY OF ADVENT: HOPE

Every Sunday of Advent the candle lighting is preceded by a brief Call to Worship

VOICE - Today is the first Sunday of Advent, the Sunday in which we recall the hope we have in Christ.

VOICE - The prophets of Israel all spoke of the coming of Christ, of how a saviour would be born, a king in the line of David. They spoke of how he would rule the world wisely and bless all nations.

VOICE - On Christmas day the Christ of our hope was born. On Good Friday the Christ of our hope died. On Easter day the Christ of our hope rose from the dead. He then ascended into heaven. On the last day, the Christ of our hope will come again to establish his kingdom over all things on earth.

VOICE - As the follower of Christ, we await his return. We light this candle to remember that as he came to us as humbly in the manger at Bethlehem and gave light to the world, so he is coming again in power to deliver his people.

VOICE - We light this candle to remind us to be alert and to watch for his return.

Light the First Candle

VOICE - LET US PRAY - Loving God, we thank you for the hope you give us. Help us prepare our hearts for the Lord's coming. Bless our worship. Help us live holy and righteous lives. We ask it in the name of the one born in Bethlehem. Amen.

THE SECOND SUNDAY OF ADVENT: PEACE

Every Sunday of Advent the candle lighting is preceded by a brief Call to Worship

VOICE - Last Sunday we lit the first candle in our Advent Wreath, the candle of hope. We light it again as we remember that Christ will come again to fulfil all of God's promises to us.

(a person lights the candle of hope)

VOICE - The second candle of Advent is the Candle of Peace. It is sometimes called the Bethlehem Candle to remind us of the place in which preparations were made to receive and cradle the Christ child.

VOICE - Peace is a gift that we must be prepared for. God gives us the gift of peace when we turn to him in faith.

VOICE - The prophet Isaiah calls Christ "the Prince of Peace." Through John the Baptist and all the other prophets, God asks us to prepare our hearts so that he may come in.

VOICE - Our hope is in God, and in his son Jesus Christ. Our peace is found in him. We light this candle today to remind us that he brings peace to all who trust in him.

Light the Second Candle

VOICE - LET US PRAY - Loving God, thank you for the peace you give us through Jesus. Help us prepare our hearts to receive Him. Bless our worship. Guide us in all that we say and do. We ask it in the name of the one born in Bethlehem. Amen.

THE THIRD SUNDAY OF ADVENT: WHITE GIFT SUNDAY - JOY

Every Sunday of Advent the candle lighting is preceded by a brief Call to Worship

VOICE - Last Sunday the candle of peace was lit. We light it and the candle of hope again as we remember that Christ will come again and bring to the world everlasting peace.

(a person lights the candles of hope, and peace.)

VOICE - The third candle of Advent is the Candle of Joy. It reminds of the joy that Mary felt when the angel Gabriel told he that a special child would be born to her- a child who would save and deliver his people.

VOICE - God wants us all to have joy. The angel who announced to the shepherds that Jesus had been born told them: "Do not be afraid. I am bringing you good news of a great joy for all people - for to you is born this day, in the City of David, a Saviour, who is the Messiah, the Lord."

VOICE - We light this candle to remember that Christ brings the promise of a new life - a life in which the blind receive sight, the lame walk, and the prisoners are set free. We light it to

remember that He is the bringer of true and everlasting joy.
Light the Third Candle

VOICE - LET US PRAY - Loving God, we thank you for the joy you bring us. Help us prepare our hearts for this gift. Bless our worship. Help us to hear and to do your word. We ask it in the name of the one born in Bethlehem. Amen.

THE FOURTH SUNDAY OF ADVENT: LOVE

Every Sunday of Advent the candle lighting is preceded by a brief Call to Worship

VOICE - Last Sunday we lit the candle of joy. We light it and the candles of hope and peace again as we remember that Christ will come again and bring us everlasting peace and joy.
(a person lights the candles of hope, peace, and joy)

VOICE - The fourth candle of Advent is the Candle of Love. Its light is meant to remind us of the love that God has for us.

VOICE - Jesus shows us God's perfect love. He is God's love in human form. The bible says that "God so loved the world that he gave his only Son, so that whoever believes in him should not perish, but have eternal life."

VOICE - Love is patient, love is kind and envies no one. Love is never boastful or conceited, rude or selfish. Love is not quick to take offence, it keeps no records of wrongs, it does not gloat over other people's troubles, but rejoices in the right, the good, and the true. There is nothing that love cannot face, there is no limit to its faith, to its hope, to its endurance. Love never ends.

VOICE - We light this candle today to remind us of how God's perfect love is found in Jesus

Light the Fourth Candle

VOICE - LET US PRAY Loving God, we thank you for your gift of love - show to us perfectly in Jesus Christ our Lord. Help us prepare our hearts to receive Him. Bless our worship. Help us to hear and do your word. We ask it in the name of the one born in Bethlehem. Amen

CHRISTMAS EVE LIGHTING THE WAY

Words of Welcome & Lighting The Advent Candles:

L= Leader; **P=People**

L: The Lord be with you.

P: And also with you.

L: We gather to celebrate the birth of the one who is the light of the world.

P: We are here to worship God - and his Son Jesus - born this night in Bethlehem of Judea.

L: *We light the candle of hope to remind us of the promises made by all the prophets that God would raise up a savior for his people Israel.*

P: Christ is our hope and our salvation. He calls us to share our hope in him with each other.

L: *We light the candle of peace to remind us that it is only with God and by following in his path that true peace can be found.*

P: Christ brings the peace of God to us. He calls us to share the peace he gives with each other.

L: *We light the candle of joy to remind us that God gives joy to every heart that abides in him.*

P: As Mary rejoiced in the birth of Jesus - so his birth in us brings us joy. God calls us to share the joy he gives with each other.

L: *We light the candle of love to remind us that Jesus is God's gift of love to us - and that in him, the light of love triumphs over darkness.*

P: Love never fails - it transforms all those who give it and receive it. God calls us to share his love with each other.

Lighting The Christ Candle

L: *We light the Christ candle to remind us that the light of the world was born this night.*

P: The people who walked in darkness have seen a great light. Those who dwelt in a land of deep darkness - on them a light has shined.

L: *You, O Lord, have multiplied the nation. You have increased its joy.*

P: For to us a child is born, to us a son is given, and the government shall be upon his shoulder.

L: *His name shall be called Wonderful Counselor, Mighty God, Everlasting Father, Prince of Peace.*

P: He is also called Emmanuel, for in him God is with us.

Unison Prayer of Approach

P: Almighty God - you have made this night holy by the gift of your son, born of the Holy Spirit and of Mary. Upon him rested all your grace, through him has come all your mercy. Let his light shine within our hearts tonight even more brightly than it shines from the candles in this place. Help us to hear your word and to celebrate your everlasting love through him. Amen

Tradition Three

The candles in some circles stand for:

- Expectation
- Bethlehem
- Shepherds
- Angels.

Tradition Four

The candles in some circles stand for:

- Expectation
- Peace
- Joy
- Love

The Wreath and its Meaning

The circle of the wreath reminds us of God Himself, His eternity and endless mercy, which has no beginning or end.

The green of the wreath speaks of the hope that we have in God, the hope of newness, of renewal, of eternal life.

Candles symbolize the light of God coming into the world through the birth of His son. The four outer candles represent the period of waiting during the four Sundays of Advent, which themselves symbolize the four centuries of waiting between the prophet Malachi and the birth of Christ.

The colors of the candles vary with different traditions, but there are usually three purple or blue candles, corresponding to the sanctuary colors of Advent, and one pink or rose candle. One of the purple candles is lighted the first Sunday of Advent, a Scripture is read, a short devotional or reading is given, and a prayer offered. On subsequent Sundays, previous candles are relit with an additional one lighted. The pink candle is lighted on the third Sunday of Advent.

The light of the candles itself becomes an important symbol of the season. The light reminds us that Jesus is the light of the world that comes into the darkness of our lives to bring newness, life, and hope.

The progression in the lighting of the candles symbolizes the various aspects of our waiting experience. As the candles are lighted over the four week period, it also symbolizes the darkness of fear and hopelessness receding and the shadows of sin falling away as more and more light is shed into the world. The flame of each new candle reminds the worshippers that something is happening, and that more is yet to come. Finally, the light that has come into the world is plainly visible as the Christ candle is lighted at Christmas, and worshippers rejoice over the fact that the promise of long ago has been realized.

Advent Calendars are another tradition as children anticipate the Christmas celebration by opening a new window, usually containing a Bible passage of prophecy, each day until Christmas.

Lutherans also traditionally have mid-week Advent services, usually on Wednesday evening, with the focus on the coming birth and a study of the prophecies of the Messiah.

Feel free to implement Advent forms in your Christmas messages. Visit on-line sites that feature Advent themes and practices. One good site is the "Christmas in Cyberspace" site—there are no Santas allowed there! The observances help to bring peace and calm and a focus on the meaning of Bethlehem's famous baby amidst the hustle and bustle of the Christmas rush.

Advent Candles: Advent 1

Hope From the Prophets

It has been a tradition in the Church to light candles during the four weeks of Advent, the season that leads up to Christmas. Advent is a Latin word meaning "to come," and for the Church serves a two-fold purpose. We await the coming of the baby in the manger like the Old Testament believers did. We also look forward to the return of our Lord on Judgment Day.

The candles are arranged in a wreath of evergreen branches. The evergreen reminds us of life even when all else has died. In like manner Christians have evergreen trees for Christmas trees. There are four candles in the circle, with a fifth white candle placed in the middle. The four candles differ in color depending upon which tradition one uses for the meaning of the candles.

One tradition has the candles represent **Hope - Peace - Joy – Love**.

Another tradition assigns to the candles the representation of **the Prophets, the Angels, the Shepherds, and the Magi**. In a sense the two traditions line up very closely with each other.

On the first week of Advent we look at the first candle lit, which can stand for Hope (a purple candle) and the Prophets (a gold candle).

The Prophets brought hope to the Old Testament believers. They brought light to a sin-darkened world. Even when the prophet was sent to foretell the destruction of a nation, imbedded in that message was the message of the coming Messiah, the Savior of the world. Often the prophets added another Messianic clue so that when the Messiah did come, the believers in Messiah's time would know Messiah had come. Even the Roman centurion on Good Friday could not help but cry out, "Surely this is the Son of God!"

We also place our hope on the Lord. The prophets justify this hope by their prophesies. The Gospel writers inform us that many of the events and miracles in Jesus' life were "just as the prophets stated." The prophets told of a Virgin birth, a birth in Bethlehem, from the line of David, that the child would be called out of Egypt and be known as a Nazarene. Yes, even the unfortunate slaughter of the Innocents of Bethlehem was prophesied!

We as New Testament Christians have the prophesies of the coming Judgment to look forward to. One can read Jesus' account in Matthew's Gospel and be frightened by what appears to be horrendous events. The book of Revelation can also have some vivid and frightening imagery. But in the end, God wins and these things will be like birth pains as we are born into eternal life in the presence of our gracious and merciful God who saved us not by what we do or who we are, but by the blood of our Lord and Savior Jesus Christ which pays for all our sins.

Advent Candles: Advent 2

A Message of Peace From the Angels

On the second week of Advent we look at the second candle lit, which can stand for Peace (a purple candle) and the Angels (a white candle).

The Angels proclaimed peace to Zachariah, Mary, Joseph, and the shepherds in the fields. They shared the Gospel message on that first Christmas, that first Noel when the angels did sing. They proclaimed that God had kept his age-old promise, first spoken to Adam and Eve right after the fall into sin but planned even before the creation of the world.

What is this peace that the angels sang about? Certainly one can look around the world and find fighting and strife. The American armed forces are currently fighting in Afghanistan and Iraq. There are threats of terror. Nations develop weapons. So how can the angels brazenly declare "peace?"

The peace the angels proclaimed was peace between God and mankind. For the birth of a baby in Bethlehem was the fulfillment of a promise to send a Savior into the world, a Savior anointed by God himself (the Messiah, the Christ). This Savior would fulfill God's Holy Law and die an innocent death to pay for the sins of the world.

We rest in peace in the Lord because of the sacrifice made by the baby in Bethlehem. The angels proclaim this inner peace for souls tormented by sin and wracked by guilt. The Gospel writers report for us that many came to find healing, comfort, and solace in the Lord of the Universe. The Church spread dramatically after the Ascension and Pentecost because of this message of peace proclaimed with a cross.

We as New Testament Christians have the peace proclaimed by the angels when we read and hear the Word of God and partake of the Sacraments. We have in intimate connection with our God and Savior because of this peace. From this peace comes peace of mind and peace with fellow believers and we seek to bring this peace to unbelievers.

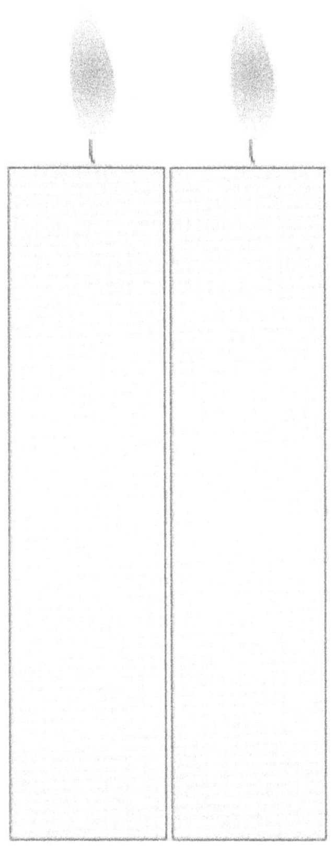

Advent Candles: Advent 3

Joy Fills the Shepherds

On the third week of Advent we look at the third candle lit, which can stand for Joy (a purple or pink candle) and the Shepherds (a green candle). The shift to the color pink can signal the shift in focus in Advent, where the first two weeks focused on the fulfillment of Old Testament prophecy and the last two weeks focus on New Testament prophecy fulfillment when Jesus returns on the Last Day.

The Shepherds received joy at the news they heard that night. Alone, in the fields watching their animals, they may have felt forsaken by God and men. Moses in fleeing the wrath of Pharoah and his conscience hides out as a shepherd. It was the shepherd boy David who was summoned from the fields to be anointed king. No doubt while Jesse made sure his sons were in attendance to meet the prophet Samuel, David was left to tend the flocks in the fields—and very likely the same fields where the Christmas shepherds were greeted by the angels!

We also receive joy from the Good Shepherd. With the guidance of the Good Shepherd we are protected, fed, watered, and cared for. He protects us—even to the point of giving up his life to give each of us life! The Good Shepherd is our Savior from sin.

The shepherds also display the joy they felt at hearing the blessed news. They ran into Bethlehem. Then they told everyone they met about what the angels said and what they saw in the manger in the stable. What a hubbub this must have created—enough that Mary treasured all these things up in her heart.

We harbor joy in the Lord because of the sacrifice made by the baby in Bethlehem. Like the shepherds we have our periods of loneliness and feeling forsaken in the desert of life. We feel empty. We feel abandoned. But the Good Shepherd brings us joy with his presence. We may not always be happy, but we are joyful. And in this joy we can say with Paul, "I do not consider the present sufferings worth comparing to the surpassing riches that will be ours in Christ."

This joy becomes our joy whenever we see and hear the Word. We hear the word of the Word in reading and hearing his message from the Bible. We see and feel the Word in the sacraments which create, strengthen, and preserve our faith in the Good Shepherd. We have joy in being redeemed and adopted as sons and daughters of the living God!

May the holiday season bring you joy and peace amid the bustle and busy-ness. Jesus, the Light of the World, is the reason for this blessed season.

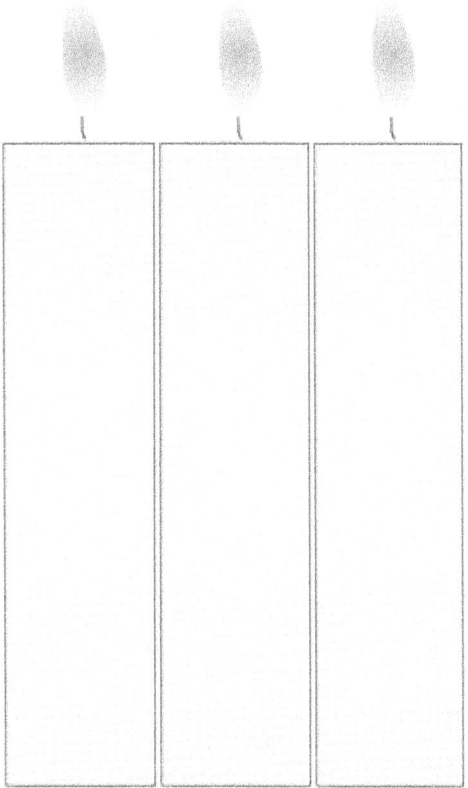

Advent Candles: Advent 4

Magi Bear Gifts in Love

The fourth week of Advent normally does not have a mid-week service. (Usually there are only three mid- week Advent services.) We look at the fourth candle lit, which can stand for Love (a purple candle) and the Magi (a blue candle).

The Magi received love by somehow knowing the strange star in the sky had an important potent. This love impelled them to travel a great distance to pay their homage to the new-born king. They bore gifts out of love for this king—a Heavenly King that loved the Magi, and all people, so much that he gave his life for the sins of all people! "Love Came Down That Christmas Day."

1 Corinthians 13:4*—Love is patient, love is kind. It does not envy, it does not boast, it is not proud.*

John 3:16*—"For God so loved the world that he gave his one and only Son,[1] that whoever believes in him shall not perish but have eternal life.*

Romans 1:7*—To all in Rome who are loved by God and called to be saints: Grace and peace to you from God our Father and from the Lord Jesus Christ.*

Romans 5:5*—And hope does not disappoint us, because God has poured out his love into our hearts by the Holy Spirit, whom he has given us.*

Romans 5:8*—But God demonstrates his own love for us in this: While we were still sinners, Christ died for us.*

Galatians 2:20*—I have been crucified with Christ and I no longer live, but Christ lives in me. The life I live in the body, I live by faith in the Son of God, who loved me and gave himself for me.*

1 John 3:1-3*—How great is the love the Father has lavished on us, that we should be called children of God! And that is what we are! The reason the world does not know us is that it did not know him. Dear friends, now we are children of God, and what we will be has not yet been made known. But we know that when he appears, we shall be like him, for we shall see him as he is. Everyone who has this hope in him purifies himself, just as he is pure.*

1 John4:7*—Dear friends, let us love one another, for love comes from God.*

Everyone who loves has been born of God and knows God. Whoever does not love does not know God, because God is love. This is how God showed his love among us: He sent his one and only Son into the world that we might live through him. This is love: not that we loved God, but that he loved us and sent his Son as an atoning sacrifice for our sins. Dear friends, since God so loved us, we also ought to love one another. No one has ever seen God; but if we love one another, God lives in us and his love is made complete in us.

We know that we live in him and he in us, because he has given us of his Spirit. And we have seen and testify that the Father has sent his Son to be the Savior of the world. If anyone acknowledges that Jesus is the Son of God, God lives in him and he in God. And so we know and rely on the love God has for us.

God is love. Whoever lives in love lives in God, and God in him. In this way, love is made complete among us so that we will have confidence on the day of judgment, because in this world we are like him. There is no fear in love. But perfect love drives out fear, because fear has to do with punishment. The one who fears is not made perfect in love.

We love because he first loved us. If anyone says, "I love God," yet hates his brother, he is a liar. For anyone who does not love his brother, whom he has seen, cannot love God, whom he has not seen. And he has given us this command: Whoever loves God must also love his brother.

You may have seen the anecdote where someone asks Jesus, "How much do you love me?" Jesus says, "This much," then stretches out his arms and dies. That is the reason for Christmas, where the God-man Jesus Christ came to die for all our sins.

May the holiday season fill you with God's love amid the bustle and busy-ness. Jesus, the Light of the World, is the reason for this blessed season.

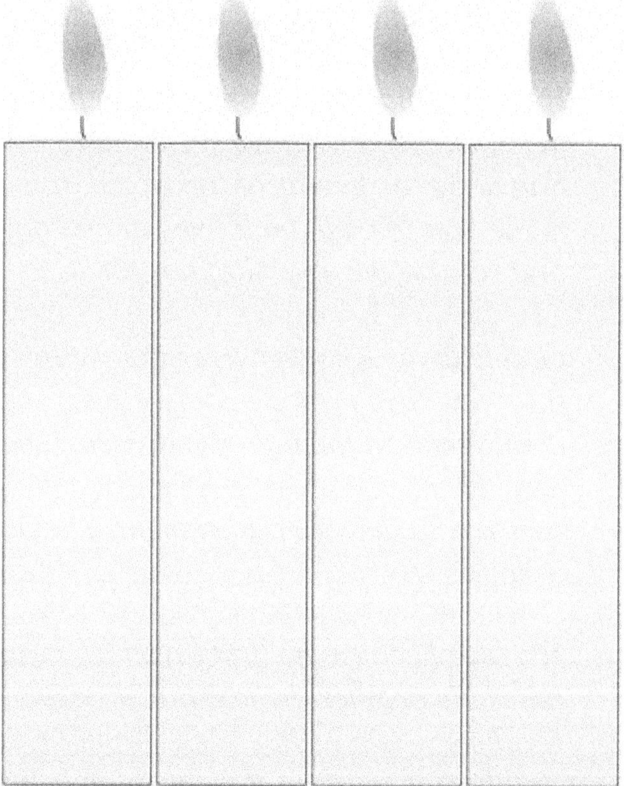

Suddenly the Lord You are Seeking Will Come to His Temple

Malachi 3: 1-4 (New International Version [NIV])
1"See, I will send my messenger, who will prepare the way before me. Then suddenly the Lord you are seeking will come to his temple; the messenger of the covenant, whom you desire, will come," says the LORD Almighty. 2But who can endure the day of his coming? Who can stand when he appears? For he will be like a refiner's fire or a launderer's soap. 3He will sit as a refiner and purifier of silver; he will purify the Levites and refine them like gold and silver. Then the LORD will have men who will bring offerings in righteousness, 4and the offerings of Judah and Jerusalem will be acceptable to the LORD, as in days gone by, as in former years.

ADVENT 2: MALACHI 3:1-4

SALEM EV. LUTHERAN CHURCH, MILWAUKEE, WI
JOHN L. HOH, JR.

Dear fellow Redeemed:

I don't know about you, but to me the month of December is one of anticipation, expectation, and wonder. There are the Christmas carols being sung that adds joy and mirth to the month. There are the gifts that one buys, anticipating the joy of the recipient. There is the anticipation of what one might receive. Then there is the food at parties, on Christmas day, even snacks as we shop.

Then suddenly it's December 25 and the culmination of the month has arrived. We have so looked forward to this day we hate to see it end. We have anticipated this day for a month—and then suddenly it's here.

That is the anticipation God told the returning exiles in Judea after the Babylonian Captivity. Through Malachi, whose name ironically means "my messenger," God says, "I will send my messenger." But this messenger isn't the prophet, but the one who will prepare the way for the Lord. God is telling us, Suddenly the Lord you are seeking will come to his temple. The Lord will refine us through his sacrifice. Because we are refined, our offerings will be acceptable.

Suddenly the Lord you are seeking will come to his temple. The Lord will refine us through his sacrifice. Of course this begs the question, "Why do I need to be refined?" Malachi's hearers obviously needed this message. Even though the nation of Judah had been in Captivity for 70 years, upon their return to Judah they fell back into old habits and patterns in their lives. The temple wasn't being built with great zeal. Imagine hearing in Malachi's words, then, when he says, "suddenly the Lord you are seeking will come to his temple"-and knowing that the progress on rebuilding the temple was behind schedule! But it is not the physical structure itself that God is worried about. Remember he used that term to refer to our bodies. He comes to us when we least expect it.

But who can endure the day of his coming? Who can stand when he appears? The Psalmist asks a similar question in Psalm 24: "Who may ascend the hill of the Lord? Who may stand in his holy place?" And when we look at our sinfulness, we realize on our own these questions are answered in the negative. We do not love God with all our hearts. We do not always help our neighbor joyfully—yes, sometimes at Christmastime we lose that joy in helping others. We seek our own pleasures before we seek our neighbor's welfare or doing God's will. Yet here is God, through Malachi, telling us he loves us and forgives us and seeks us to be his own. How can God do this?

God does this by refining us. The Lord comes to refine us as a refiner refines gold or silver or any other metal. Ore comes as a rock with the metal in it. The process of refining means usually the large ore rocks need to be broken down, then extreme heat applied to separate the metal from the slag. It is then that the metal is refined and can be fashioned into something useful. God carries out this process of refinement in us. This process began when Jesus died on the cross to pay for all our sins. This process continues as the Holy Spirit works to create and strengthen faith in our hearts. This process occurs throughout our life as our Lord works in our lives to refine us, to make us holy, to work in us for works of service. And in the process of refinement we can endure his coming and to stand when he appears.

There was a ladies Bible study group that had studied a passage in Scripture about a refiner refining silver, much like Malachi tells us in our text this evening. They wished to know more about this process, so they looked for a silversmith in the phone book, they found one, and made an appointment to visit his workshop. As the ladies watched, the silversmith melted the ore with such great heat that the silversmith sweated profusely and the ladies needed to stand far back. The melted ore induced slag to float to the top where it could be removed as the silver was purified.

As the ladies thanked the silversmith and were leaving, one lady asked, "How do you know when the silver is purified perfectly?"

"That's easy," answered the silversmith. "It's purified when I can see my reflection in it."

Suddenly the Lord you are seeking will come to his temple. Because we are refined, our offerings will be acceptable. The process of refinement is what gives us the right to stand before our Lord. It is also what makes our sacrifices acceptable before God. This process is lifelong and not complete until we enter eternity. Until then, like Paul we "see through a glass darkly." We reflect God's image better and better as we are guided through life by God and he refines us as one would refine silver.

Because of Christ and his sacrifice, we can now offer sacrifices pleasing to God. Malachi tells us, "the offerings of Judah and Jerusalem will be acceptable to the Lord."

In this we have a picture of the Church whose sacrifices are pleasing to God because of what the Lord who has suddenly come has done. Just as sacrifices were acceptable "from days gone by, as in former years." Remember, Malachi's hearers are still trying to rebuild the temple. The sacrifices had ceased. But new sacrifices-not animal sacrifices, but sacrifices of broken and contrite hearts and repentant believers-will be made in righteousness. But how can we make sacrifices in righteousness?

Habakkuk tells us "the righteous will live by his faith." Paul quotes this verse from Habakkuk no less than three times in his letters. This verse gives us insight into how we make sacrifices in righteousness. We make these sacrifices in faith, believing and trusting that the Lord whom we sought has suddenly come, has taken our place, and has paid the price for our sins.

This Lord, whom we seek, was foretold by the prophets. Micah in our reading this evening gave us some clues about this coming. "But you, Bethlehem Ephrathah, though you are small among the clans of Judah, out of you will come for me one who will be ruler over Israel." Micah tells us that this Lord will originate in Bethlehem. Micah goes on, "whose origins are from of old, from ancient times." This echoes David's psalm when he says, "The Lord said to my Lord, 'sit at my right hand until I put your enemies under your feet'." Jesus himself said, "Before Abraham was, I Am." That baby that we will find in a manger existed before the creation of the world and helped in that creation.

Micah goes on, "He will shepherd his flock in the strength of the Lord and in the majesty of the name of the LORD his God. And they will live securely, for then his greatness will reach to the ends of the earth. And he will be their peace." David in Psalm 23 tells us, "The LORD is my shepherd, I shall not want." Jesus takes this title when he says, "I Am the Good Shepherd." Jesus shepherds us in strength and majesty through the valleys of the shadow of death and to green pastures and still waters. This greatness will reach the ends of the earth, to "every land, nation, and tribe." And by his sacrifice, Jesus makes himself our peace with God, even as the angels sang about this "peace on earth to men on whom his favor rests."

Soon, December 25 and its excitement will be here and gone. The days after will find us back in our daily routines. Another December 25 will seem a long way off. But the message and meaning of that first Christmas Day and its implications for our lives, here and in eternity, will remain. For the Lord we sought has come and will come again. We are refined through the sacrifice of the Lord and that refinement makes us, and our sacrifices, acceptable to God. This is what the prophets foretold and what the Prophet greater than Moses fulfilled.

The Impatient Advent Christian

Come Here NOW, Immanuel

As Christians we want the end to come soon. Many even now see world events with terrorism, wars, shootings, abortion, and a whole host of other societal ills and match them up with what Jesus says in Matthew's Gospel:

> *Jesus left the temple and was walking away when his disciples came up to him to call his attention to its buildings. "Do you see all these things?" he asked. "I tell you the truth, not one stone here will be left on another; every one will be thrown down."*
>
> *As Jesus was sitting on the Mount of Olives, the disciples came to him privately. "Tell us," they said, "when will this happen, and what will be the sign of your coming and of the end of the age?"*
>
> *Jesus answered: "Watch out that no one deceives you. For many will come in my name, claiming, 'I am the Christ,' and will deceive many. You will hear of wars and rumors of wars, but see to it that you are not alarmed. Such things must happen, but the end is still to come. Nation will rise against nation, and kingdom against kingdom. There will*

be famines and earthquakes in various places. All these are the beginning of birth pains.
"Then you will be handed over to be persecuted and put to death, and you will be hated by all nations because of me. At that time many will turn away from the faith and will betray and hate each other, and many false prophets will appear and deceive many people. Because of the increase of wickedness, the love of most will grow cold, but he who stands firm to the end will be saved. And this gospel of the kingdom will be preached in the whole world as a testimony to all nations, and then the end will come.

"So when you see standing in the holy place 'the abomination that causes desolation,' spoken of through the prophet Daniel—let the reader understand—then let those who are in Judea flee to the mountains. Let no one on the roof of his house go down to take anything out of the house. Let no one in the field go back to get his cloak. How dreadful it will be in those days for pregnant women and nursing mothers! Pray that your flight will not take place in winter or on the Sabbath. For then there will be great distress, unequaled from the beginning of the world until now—and never to be equaled again. If those days had not been cut short, no one would survive, but for the sake of the elect those days will be shortened. At that time if anyone says to you, 'Look, here is the Christ!' or, 'There he is!' do not believe it. For false Christs and false prophets will appear and perform great signs and miracles to deceive even the elect—If that were possible.

See, I have told you ahead of time.

"So if anyone tells you, 'There he is, out in the desert,' do not go out; or, 'Here he is, in the inner rooms,' do not believe it. For as lightning that comes from the east is visible even in the west, so will be the coming of the Son of Man. 28Wherever there is a carcass, there the vultures will gather.

"Immediately after the distress of those days
" 'the sun will be darkened,
and the moon will not give its light;
the stars will fall from the sky,
and the heavenly bodies will be shaken.'

"At that time the sign of the Son of Man will appear in the sky, and all the nations of the earth will mourn. They will see the Son of Man coming on the clouds of the sky, with power and great glory. And he will send his angels with a loud trumpet call, and they will gather his elect from the four winds, from one end of the heavens to the other.

"Now learn this lesson from the fig tree: As soon as its twigs get tender and its leaves come out, you know that summer is near. Even so, when you see all these things, you know that it is near, right at the door. I tell you the truth, this generation will certainly not pass away until all these things have happened. Heaven and earth will pass away, but my words will never pass away.

"No one knows about that day or hour, not even the angels in heaven, nor the Son, but only the Father. As it was in the days of Noah, so it will be at the coming of the Son of Man. For in the days before the flood, people were eating and drinking, marrying and giving in marriage, up to the day Noah entered the ark; and they knew nothing about what would happen until the flood came and took them all away. That is how it will be at the coming of the Son of Man. Two men will be in the field; one will be taken and the other left. Two women will be grinding with a hand mill; one will be taken and the other left.

"Therefore keep watch, because you do not know on what day your Lord will come. But understand this: If the owner of the house had known at what time of night the thief was coming, he would have kept watch and would not have let his house be broken into. So you also must be ready, because the Son of Man will come at an hour when you do not expect him.

"Who then is the faithful and wise servant, whom the master has put in charge of the servants in his household to give them their food at the proper time? It will be good for that servant whose master finds him doing so when he returns. I tell you the truth, he will put him in charge of all his possessions. But suppose that servant is wicked and says to himself, 'My master is staying away a long time,' and he then begins to beat his fellow servants and to eat and drink with drunkards. The master of that servant will

> *come on a day when he does not expect him and at an hour he is not aware of. He will cut him to pieces and assign him a place with the hypocrites, where there will be weeping and gnashing of teeth. (Matthew 24)*

Why do we have this fascination with the end of the world? For one, we recognize we are merely Pilgrims here. God is preparing a better home for us. We don't know what it will be like, but I have a hunch that we will not lack anything. Jesus often referred to heaven as "like a feast." (One seminary professor told us that maybe the song "In Heaven There is No Beer" was false theology because Jesus always pictured heaven as a feast and any good German knows that without beer the meal cannot be a feast.)

When I visited shut-ins, there would be some that asked why God took so long in calling them home. These Pilgrims were convinced that their days of useful service were over and they wanted their heavenly rest. Now, I guess you *can* convince yourself that you are useless if you are in a confined area called a nursing home and ultimately have to be fed, bathed, and other bodily functions handled by someone else. But another seminary professor told us another truth. These people now have time. They can pray! So I began taking prayer lists to these people. If you want to see someone in a dreary situation with a depressing attitude perk up and come back to life, entrust them with the important job of being your congregation's and country's ambassador to God! You think Pollyanna did a miracle on Mrs. Snow, you'll be amazed at the one you'll initiate.

You see, people want to be useful. And if you're stuck in a "human warehouse" awaiting the inevitable, then one's spirit flags and depression sets in. It is a hopeless feeling.

But now prayer, and on behalf of church and country at that, can be a real pick-me-up and give a person a profound sense of importance.

Prayer is a panacea, not only for the shut-in, but for the church and nation as well. All those societal ills around us we can mark as signs of our Lord's coming and leave it at that. Unfortunately, people are suffering because of these ills. But by having believers pray for these things gets them thinking. And sometimes in thinking, Christians are led to find creative solutions and maybe not handle the "big picture" problem but a part of it in their own little world in their own little way. It begins the "1000 Points of Light" that George H. W. Bush once commented on.

Impatience is a part of human existence. It is part of our sinful nature. Children cannot wait for Christmas. Adults cannot wait for the next paycheck. And often as Christians we cannot wait for God's deliverance in our lives. But patiently we must wait for God has his timeline and he will not be hurried. The Old Testament believers waited millennia for the Messiah; we can wait his return.

Join me this Advent season for a light-hearted look at our impatience as Christians.

Lord, I Want Patience and I Want it NOW

No doubt many of you have heard that age old joke where an impatient person prays, “Lord, please give me patience and give it to me **now**!” We can smile at the disparity of the request and the nature of the request.

This impatience is a facet of the sinful human condition. Anyone with small children well know the impatience of children. Go for a trip and after ten minutes the back seat chorus goes, “Are we there yet?” In fact, my son has a Simpson’s watch that has the following dialogue in rapid-fire succession:
Children: “Are we there yet?”
Homer: “No”
Children: “Are we there yet?”
Homer: “No”
Children: “Are we there yet?” Homer: “No”

NOTE: I’m not sure how Matthew got this watch, but when I find out *who* gave him that watch, you can bet I can get an equally annoying gift for *their* child(ren).

Children will also get up at the “crack of dawn” on Christmas morning. Why? There are presents beneath the tree! Who wants to stay in bed when there are presents under the tree?

It takes some practice to curb one’s impatience in such times. No doubt a chilly home in the winter prompts us to keep snuggled under blankets and quilts as long as possible on a day when we have no obligations. Or even loneliness. I had a great aunt who would collect her presents every Christmas. Mind you, she never opened them in front of us. She would just look at the brightly wrapped packages and thank each person who gave her a gift. The gifts would still be unwrapped when Dad or Grandpa took her home in the evening. As a child, I thought this was odd behavior. But, you see, she lived alone and was in her 80's and 90's (she joined the Church Triumphant at the age of 95). She would proceed to open *one* package each day until the packages were all opened. Can you imagine getting a child to do that?

But we live in an impatient world. A business no longer needs to make the best, it just has to be first into the marketplace. We want immediate gratification **now**. We eat on the run. We use freeways to get to our destinations faster. Ah, for the days when families took a leisurely drive and read the Burma-Shave signs:

> *For this Christmas Slow down and wait. / Take a breath,/ Exhale, / anticipate, / Then celebrate. / He-Came-to-Save.*

Maybe we can Burma-Shave the holidays?

> *God's own Son / Came down this day. / As a baby, / He came down, / Our sins to pay. / Triune God.*

> *In a manger / Full of hay./ Mary laid Jesus / In swaddling clothes / And arms of love. / God the Father.*
>
> *The angels sang/ In the Judean hills / A baby born / Promised of old / To heal our ills. / Judean Shepherds.*
>
> *Wise men came / So long ago./ A star they followed / From the East / With much ado. / We Three Kings.*

Let the patient peace of this Christmas season settle in your hearts. This Promise took several millennia for God to fulfill, but in his time he fulfilled it. We might find the wait for his return disconcerting, but wait patiently we must. We will get to heaven soon enough. And since eternity never ends, what's the rush?

Why Do I Have to Wait So Long?

Advent means “to come.” Inherent in that word is the sense that something anticipated hasn’t yet come. As Christians we observe two periods of anticipation. First, we observe the anticipation of the Old Testament believers who clung to the promise made by God in the Garden of Eden that he would send a Savior, born of a woman, to free us from our sins. For several millennia God’s people from every nation awaiting the fulfillment of that promise.

As Christians we also observe our own anticipation. We anticipate when our king will “come again” and fulfill his promise to gather us together to the heavenly mansion. Thus our Advent observances have an “End Times” aspect to them.

One might wonder why God didn’t just send his Son right after the Fall into sin and get this all over with right away. Come to think of it, he could have ended the world with its sin and misery as well. Ah, but how would we have truly known the love of God! How could we know that he loves us and will take care of us?

The early Christians also eagerly awaited the second coming. In John’s Revelation we observe the “Great White Host” call out: “How long, Sovereign Lord, holy and true, until you judge the inhabitants of the earth and avenge our blood?” (John 6:10) John goes on to report to us: “Then each of them was given a white robe, and they were told to wait a little longer, until the number of their fellow servants and brothers who were to be killed as they had been was completed.”

I have always been fascinated by this verse. In this verse John sees those who had been slain in the name of the Lamb that was slain. When John received his vision the Apostle Paul likely was part of that assembly. I have always wondered at that irony, for if God hadn't been patient with people Paul may not have been converted and ultimately become part of that assembly.

(As a note, this is speculation on my part. John is not told who may or who may not have been assembled. And it is a vision, lest we read too much into the account. I am merely surmising that irony may exist in this vision.)

God is definitely patient. In Genesis we read:

> *As the sun was setting, Abram fell into a deep sleep, and a thick and dreadful darkness came over him. Then the LORD said to him, "Know for certain that your descendants will be strangers in a country not their own, and they will be enslaved and mistreated four hundred years. But I will punish the nation they serve as slaves, and afterward they will come out with great possessions. You, however, will go to your fathers in peace and be buried at a good old age. In the fourth generation your descendants will come back here, for the sin of the Amorites has not yet reached its full measure."*
>
> *(Genesis 15:12-16)*

Many see the genocide in the Old Testament as an act of an angry and vengeful God. But look closely and you'll notice that he is giving the

Canaanites 400 years of grace! Well, except for Sodom and Gomorrah, which will see fire and brimstone before long. But read about the depravity of these two cities and you get a sense of what the inhabitants of the land of Canaan were already like. Yet God is giving them another 400 years.

Before the Flood God was equally gracious. The evil actions of people are already enraging God. But he selects Noah to build an ark to preserve a remnant of creation. And he allows the construction of an ark for 160 years. Almost sounds like a government project, no? Maybe Noah had to get building permits and an ark license. Who knows. But primarily God is extending his time of grace another 160 years before sending the water rushing and raging over the earth (with even the water below earth's surface breaking through, it would appear). Of course, there may have been more believers than Noah, his wife, their three sons and their wives. God no doubt took believers home to be with him through the flood or just prior to the flood. I remember seeing several timelines of the patriarchs up to the Flood and several of these have Methuselah dying the year the Flood came. Of course this assumes there are no gaps in the genealogy in Genesis.

And no doubt as we live out our lives we see a society around us scorning our values and morals. God, why do you keep this earth going with the sinfulness around us? Why do we have to keep suffering? Many elderly parishioners have looked with longing for their eternal home. My grandfather would say in his final years, "They can come with the hearse and take me away anytime now." Just before he passed away, he said to grandma, "I'm going to go be with mama now." He was 16 when his mother died; he died at the age of 91. He waited longingly to be reunited with his mother.

End Times

One focus of Advent is on the New Testament believer's anticipation of the coming of our Lord to Judge and Rule the world on the last day. This chapter looks at the End Times aspect of our Advent expectation.

The church year is now drawing to a close. Following on the heels of Thanksgiving comes the Advent season which kicks off a new Church year. Thus the Sundays of Pentecost draw to a close.

The final three Sundays of Pentecost are known as the Sundays of the End Times. In these weeks we look at what Scripture says about the coming end of the world, the last Judgment, and our eternal life as part of the Great White Host.

And well the end of the Church Year should focus on the End Times, for Pentecost observes our lives in Christ. And what other terminus does a life in Christ have other than anticipating his return, preparing for heaven, and living eternally with our Lord in heaven with his

Father?

In celebrating the End Times, we are celebrating the coming of our King to gather us to heavenly mansions. Advent's focus on the coming King also has a taste of End Times in it. Good planning will prevent the focus of end times from dragging out to seven total weeks.

Within the End Times time frame in the Church Year is Reformation, when we celebrate that we have an inheritance that is ours through grace by faith alone. Thanksgiving, though a secular holiday, falls in the End Times period and reminds us to give thanks to God for his gift of salvation even as we await his coming, or him calling us home to eternal rest.

A favorite hymn of mine is "Behold a Host, Arrayed in White." Based on the vision of Saint John in Revelation of the Great White Host in heaven, the hymn is a joyous celebration of the eternal life awaiting us in heaven. It is a hymn that will be sung at my funeral, if I die before the Lord's return.

During this time we can repeat the Easter greeting of the ancient Christians: "Allelujah! Christ has Risen! He has risen indeed! Allelulah!" Easter is a major componenet of the End Times, because if Christ did not rise, we are still in our sins and we have no hope after death. Christ's resurrection means that the End Times and the Judgment are not to be feared, but rather are, as Matthew quotes Jesus, "Like birth pains." Any mother will tell you that the pain of childbirth is forgotten once the mother holds her child for the first time. Our travails here on earth will be forgotten amid the joys of heaven.

"Behold a Host, Arrayed in White" by Hans A. Brorson, 1694-1764
Text From: *The Lutheran Hymnal* (St. Louis: Concordia Publishing House, 1941)

1. Behold a host, arrayed in white,
Like thousand snow-clad mountains bright, With palms they stand.
Who is this band
Before the throne of light?
Lo, these are they of glorious fame Who from the great affliction came And in the flood of Jesus' blood
Are cleansed from guilt and blame. Now gathered in the holy place, Their voices they in worship raise,
Their anthems swell where God doth dwell, Mid angels' songs of praise.

2. Despised and scorned, they sojourned here; But now, how glorious they must appear! Those martyrs stand a priestly band, God's throne forever near.
So oft, in troubled days gone by,
In anguish they would weep and sigh, At home above the God of Love
For aye their tears shall dry.
They now enjoy their Sabbath rest, The paschal banquet of the blest;
The Lamb, their Lord, at festal board
Himself is Host and Guest.

3. Then hail, ye mighty legions, yea, All hail! Now safe and blest

for aye,
And praise the Lord, who with His Word
Sustained you on the way.
Ye did the joys of earth disdain,
Ye toiled and sowed in tears and pain. Farewell, now bring your sheaves and sing Salvation's glad refrain.
Swing high your palms, lift up your song,
Yea, make it myriad voices strong, Eternally shall praise to Thee,
God, and the Lamb belong.

Notes:
Hymn #656 from *The Lutheran Hymnal*
Text: Revelation 7:13-17
Author: Hans Adolf Brorson, c. 1760
Translated by: composite
Titled: "Den store hvide Flok vi se" Norwegian folk-tune, c. 1600
Tune: "Great White Host"
Arranged by: Edvard H. Grieg, 1907, ad.

Congregational Setting

1.

CONGREGATION: Behold a host, arrayed in white, Like thousand snow-clad mountains bright,
With palms they stand.
Who is this band
Before the throne of light?

CHOIR: Lo, these are they of glorious fame
Who from the great affliction came
And in the flood of Jesus' blood
Are cleansed from guilt and blame. Now gathered in the holy place, Their voices they in worship raise,
Their anthems swell where God doth dwell,
Mid angels' songs of praise.

2.

PASTOR: Despised and scorned, they sojourned here;
But now, how glorious they must appear!
Those martyrs stand a priestly band,
God's throne forever near.
So oft, in troubled days gone by,
In anguish they would weep and sigh, At home above the God of Love
For aye their tears shall dry.
They now enjoy their Sabbath rest, The paschal banquet of the blest;
The Lamb, their Lord, at festal board
Himself is Host and Guest.

3.

CONGREGATION: Then hail, ye mighty legions, yea, All hail!
Now safe and blest for aye,
And praise the Lord, who with His Word
Sustained you on the way.
Ye did the joys of earth disdain,
Ye toiled and sowed in tears and pain.
Farewell, now bring your sheaves and sing
Salvation's glad refrain.
Swing high your palms, lift up your song,
Yea, make it myriad voices strong, Eternally
shall praise to Thee,
God, and the Lamb belong.

Verse Three can be sung antiphonally.

www.ingramcontent.com/pod-product-compliance
Ingram Content Group UK Ltd.
Pitfield, Milton Keynes, MK11 3LW, UK
UKHW051136260726
13967UKWH00010B/3077

9 781105 257216